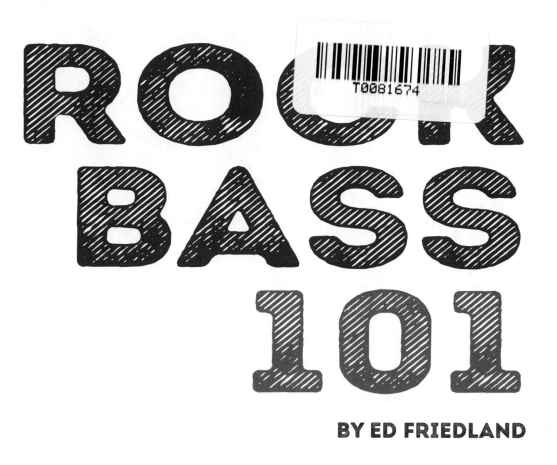

ROCK BASS 101

BY ED FRIEDLAND

PLAYBACK+
Speed • Pitch • Balance • Loop

To access audio visit:
www.halleonard.com/mylibrary

Enter Code
3900-0803-8131-9483

ISBN: 978-1-5400-2668-2

HAL•LEONARD®

Visit Hal Leonard Online at
www.halleonard.com

Contact Us:
Hal Leonard
7777 West Bluemound Road
Milwaukee, WI 53213
Email: info@halleonard.com

In Europe contact:
Hal Leonard Europe Limited
Distribution Centre, Newmarket Road
Bury St Edmunds, Suffolk, IP33 3YB
Email: info@halleonardeurope.com

In Australia contact:
Hal Leonard Australia Pty. Ltd.
4 Lentara Court
Cheltenham, Victoria, 3192 Australia
Email: info@halleonard.com.au

TABLE OF CONTENTS

INTRODUCTION

The term "rock music" describes everything from Elvis Presley to Imagine Dragons, so how can one book teach you how to play rock bass? It's simple. A bass player in any style of rock—or even better, any style of *music*—has the same job description:

1. Play the root of the chord.
2. Keep the tempo steady.
3. Play rhythms that support and define the groove.
4. Keep the form of the song intact.

Bass playing—particularly rock bass playing—doesn't have to be complicated. In fact, most experienced bass players will tell you that simpler is better. The good news is, you can learn enough to be a "functioning" bass player and get in a band very quickly. The bad news is, many players never go beyond the absolute entry level of playing, and spend their entire musical lives with no clue about what they're doing or how to get better. You don't have to be a musical genius or theory geek to be a good bass player, but learning about the notes you play will help you build solid bass lines of your own. You'll *feel* the music even deeper because it's not just wiggling your fingers in the right spots, you'll know the *music*.

HOW IT WORKS

This book starts with some basic technique study to get your hands feeling natural on the bass, as well as helping you to learn the fingerboard. Rather than just throwing you a couple of cool licks, this book will show you the most important concepts for constructing a solid bass line, and how to find options. You'll learn how to create your own bass lines using a wide range of musical ideas, and best of all—you'll know why they work. This book also shows you some classic, must-know bass patterns that work for all types of music, and how to use them.

This book will place some reasonable demands on you as a learner. It will force you to think and discover things for yourself. Don't be frightened off because every note isn't written in tablature—tab is helpful, and we will use it for some things, but the goal here is to make you a self-sufficient bass player, not just someone that has to follow the guitar player's left hand all the time. To be that, you'll have to know your instrument, the music, and what you need to play. This book will show you a musical idea, then give you a chance to use it—for yourself. The examples without specific written bass lines are there for you to create your own part—which is what people expect you know how to do. Once you've absorbed the material in this book, you'll have everything you need to be a *real* bass player, one who understands what they're doing and can come up with the perfect line for any musical situation—on the spot.

ACKNOWLEDGMENTS

I'd like to thank Jeff Schroedl for seeing the value in this material, and to Dawn Friedland for her undying love and support. Thanks to all my editors, past and present, at *Bass Player* magazine for helping me become a better writer, and special thanks to all the great bassists that inspired me to play, and ultimately dedicate my life to music.

USING THE AUDIO

The audio that comes with this book will be your band. Playing bass by yourself is necessary when you're learning something, but when it's time to put those ideas into action, you need a band to hear how they work. The music uses a split mix with the drums, guitars and keyboards in the left channel, and the bass in the right. This lets you hear the bass part clearly so you can learn it, and allows you to remove it and play with the other instruments on your own.

Each example in the book with an icon 🔊 next to it has a number that corresponds to the audio track number. Each example will have a two-measure count-off: two half notes and three quarter notes, leaving beat four blank. For example: 1...2...1, 2, 3, (4).. (play).

If the tempo is too fast, spend some time working through the notes out of tempo. When you know the line better, use **PLAYBACK+** to slow down the audio without changing the key. While the examples are written to demonstrate the specific idea being discussed, any audio track can be used to practice any idea we talk about. There are also some full-length tunes in the back that will give you the chance to test your physical and mental stamina.

ABOUT THE NOTATION

Most of the rock-oriented bass books you see are written with tablature (or *tab* for short). Contrary to what some teachers feel, tab is not evil! However, it does have a tendency to keep you from looking for other ways to play something. For most of this book, we're going to do it a little differently. Tab gives you fret numbers on individual strings to show you exactly WHERE to play the notes on the neck of the bass. That's fine at first, but there is always more than one way to play any given bass line; the same note can show up in as many as four different locations on a four-string bass. Even if you only have two choices, it's in your best interest to know them both. Rather than tab out every possible way for you to play something, I'm going to help you understand your fingerboard well enough so you can find these alternatives yourself. That is one of the big differences between a bass player and a *bassist*. Anyone who picks up a bass and plunks out a sound is technically a bass *player*. But someone who has an understanding of what they're doing with the instrument is a *bassist*.

The "delivery system" for this information will be fairly simple: you'll see fingerboard grids laying out the names of the notes in different places on the neck, this will give you a visual reference point to find the bass line in other positions. You'll learn the various major scale positions, and the numerical system that identifies each note in the scale. The scale numbers will teach you to look at the bass line in a generic, "portable" way, making it easier to find the patterns throughout the fingerboard, and transpose them to new keys instantly. The bass lines will be written in standard notation, and underneath each note will be a scale number or a group of letters describing what that note is doing. (For example, *chr* would mean the note above is a chromatic approach.) These markings show you how the bass line is constructed, which helps you find different ways to play it, move it to another key, another song, or another band. So get prepared for a very different approach to learning the bass. This book will not "chew your food for you," but it will challenge you to learn something about the instrument you've chosen to play, and teach you the skills that people really need from a bass player in a band.

PART 1
Some Basic Tips on Playing

This book is not really about how to play bass; it's about learning what to play. But many of you have never played before, so don't skip these beginning exercises. To make it simple, here are a few suggestions accompanied by pictures—I'm told they're worth a thousand words.

Find a comfortable height for the bass. It's important not to strain any part of your body while playing; tension and strain can lead to physical problems like tendonitis, carpal tunnel, and other fun stuff. Holding the bass too low creates an extreme bend in the left wrist and limits your ability to move freely on the fingerboard. On the other hand, putting the bass up too high results in an extreme bend in the right wrist, which puts pressure on the right hand. You may also feel your right shoulder getting stiff from being scrunched up. Find a middle position (Photo 1) where you have good access to the bass neck with the left hand, and a relaxed bend in the right hand. This will allow you to play for long periods of time without pain.

Photo 1. Just Right

The Right Hand Position

Let the fingers of your right hand fall naturally over the strings (see Photo 2); don't curl them up, or force them out straight. Start by resting your thumb on the top of the pickup, but don't get too anchored there—you'll be moving it soon. Play the string by putting the tip of the pad of your finger on top of the string (see photo 3) and pulling down and across the string. Don't pluck the string from underneath.

Photo 2

Photo 3

First, just pluck the string with your first finger only, a lot of playing can be done this way. Next, alternate between the first and second fingers and play the E string repeatedly. Each finger is slightly different, so getting consistent volume and tone will require you to adjust the amount of fingertip and strength you use. Eventually, you'll develop a feel for each string and how it responds—the key is to *listen* to the sound you produce! Make your adjustments based on what you hear, not what you think.

Play Example A. If you're playing with a metronome, or click, dial in a tempo around 90 bpm (beats per minute). The note value of each note is a *half* note, which gets two clicks or beats. If 90 bpm is too fast, play it slower to make sure you produce a clean sound from each note, and keep the steady tempo.

Ex. A. Open E String

Move across to the A string now. Again, put the pad of the fingertip on top of the string and pull down and across—you'll find that as the strings get thinner, it helps to use a little more "flesh" to keep the sound even. The finger should come to rest against the E string at the end of the stroke. This helps keep the E string from ringing and insures that you're getting the proper angle of "attack" on the string.

Photo 4. End of Stroke

Play Example B on the open A string, with the same attention to detail that you used on the E string.

Ex. B. Open A String

Photo 5. Drop the Thumb

When playing the D string, drop your thumb so that it rests on the E string (see Photo 5). This accomplishes two things: it mutes the E string, and it helps preserve the proper angle of attack on the D string. Keeping the angle of attack consistent leads to a consistent tone. As with the A string, you may want to use a little more fingertip on the D string, as it's thinner and has less bottom to the sound. Practice Example C.

Ex. C. Open D String

Playing the G string requires you to mute both the E and A strings. You can do this one of two ways: you can drop the thumb onto the A string and lean it against the E string (Photo 6)...

Photo 6

...or you can keep the thumb on the E string and use your ring finger to mute the A. This may be a little tricky at first, but it's worth learning. If you ever move up to a five-string bass, you'll need to use both muting techniques to keep your bass quiet when you play the G string.

Photo 7

Being the skinniest string on the bass, you'll definitely want to use more "meat" on the G string to fatten the sound, and keep it in balance with the E string. Start the stroke with the string placed roughly behind where your fingernail starts. Play Example D.

Ex. D. Open G String

Beat: 1	2	3	4	1	2	3	4

The Left Hand Position

Proper left hand position will allow you to play the bass with greater flexibility. While there is a well-established tradition of players using the "monkey grip" on the neck, it greatly limits your ability to play more complicated lines. We're going to learn to play with "good" technique first: this way you can choose what works best for the line and let your technique adapt itself to the demands of the music. Pounding away on the root may not require perfect technique, but playing a cool fill might!

Keep your thumb low on the neck, and parallel with the frets.

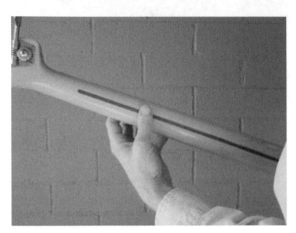

Photo 8

Let your fingers stay open and relaxed over the strings; don't force them to stretch open or cram them together.

Photo 9

The Chromatic Warm-Up Exercise

Here's a great warm-up exercise that works the left and right hands together. It's simple to remember, and it'll help you develop your coordination and timing when practiced with a metronome. There are two popular fingering systems for the left hand, the 1–2–4 system, and the 1–2–3–4 or "one finger per fret" system. You'll need to be comfortable with both because certain lines work better with one or the other—the goal is to keep your left hand as stress-free as possible. This exercise (Ex. E) works with the 1–2–4 fingering system. Starting with each open string, place your index finger on the first fret,

Photo 10

your middle finger on the second fret, and your pinky on the third fret. The ring finger just chills out and does nothing! You'll really notice the benefit of this system in the lower part of the fingerboard (which is where we *live*!) For an experiment, play the low F (first fret E string) with your index finger and the low G (third fret E string) with your ring finger. Kinda sucks, huh? Now imagine repeating those two notes over and over for about five minutes. You get the picture?

Ex. E. The Chromatic Warm-Up Exercise 1–2–4 Version

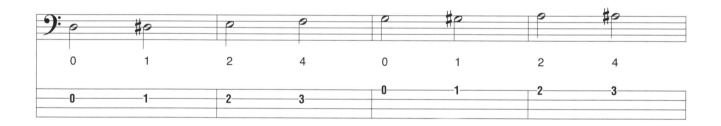

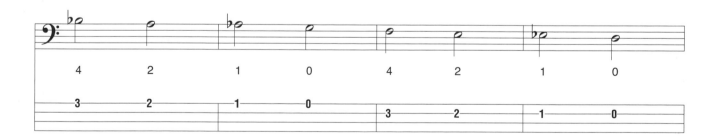

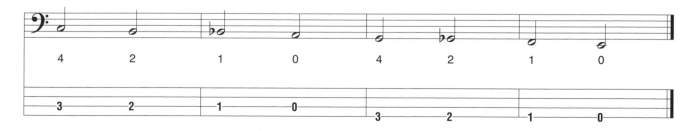

This next exercise works with the "one-finger-per-fret" fingering system. It's the method we use for playing lines that include scale and chromatic runs. One common mistake players make is to try to stretch their fingers out to "meet" the frets. Rather than forcing your fingers apart, *pivot* with the thumb in between playing with the second and third fingers. This will eliminate stress when you play. Never force the hand; tension will always cause problems.

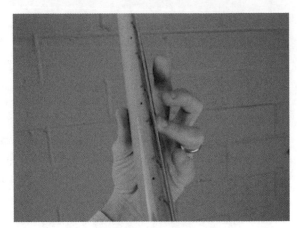

Photo 11. The Pivot

Ex. F. The Chromatic Warm-Up Exercise "One-Finger-Per-Fret" Version

Once you've completed this pattern, move it up one fret and repeat. Continue moving up one fret until you hit the seventh fret, then change directions and move it down one fret each time. Pay attention to the tone and volume of each note. Even though you're focused on the left hand, don't let the right hand slip into bad habits. Remember to mute the E and A strings with the thumb as you move to the D and G.

Let's Add the Metronome

Now that your hands are comfortable with this exercise, let's take it to the next level. Adding a metronome will help you develop your timekeeping. Why is this important? Because ultimately, it doesn't matter how fast you can play, how clever your ideas are, or how cool you look with your bass; if you can't keep time, you are essentially worthless as a bass player! Harsh words, but true words. Keeping time and making the music groove are the most important parts of your job. In my book *Bass Grooves* (Backbeat Books), I go into great detail about time keeping, internalizing rhythm, and a wide range of groove-related topics. When you're ready to dig deeper into the art of the groove, dig there.

For now, let's start with something simple. For every note you play in the previous chromatic exercise, let the metronome click twice. (Technically, that makes them *half* notes). Start between 60-80 bpm, and stay focused on the tempo. Are you speeding up? Well, then...chill out, relax, and LISTEN. Are you slowing down? Then get on the bus man, don't be left behind! LISTEN! That's the key to success in all areas of music—listening.

The Root–Five–Octave Exercise

Another very important fingering pattern to learn is the *root–five–octave* (or R–5–8) position. These three notes (the root or "1," the 5th or "5," and the octave or "8") form the foundation of bass playing in all styles of music.

The R–5–8 position forms what I call the *box shape*, and uses the 1–2–4 fingering system. The box shape helps save strain on the left hand when you're playing repetitive octave-type lines. Play the root with the first finger and the 5th with the fourth finger. Keep the first knuckle of the fourth finger arched a bit, and play a little more on the tip.

Photo 12

Photo 13

To play the octave, flatten out the knuckle of your fourth finger and roll across to the next string, playing the note with more of the finger pad. It's a little tricky at first, but once you get the hang of it, your playing will flow. We bassists play up and down the R–5–8 all the time, so you'll need to get used to it.

Here's a great exercise to help you get the R–5–8 position working. Practice it slowly to get your hands comfortable with the "pinky roll." Once you have the mechanics of the exercise smooth, play it with a metronome, starting around 50-60 bpm. The first two notes of the measure are quarter notes— they get one click each. The third note is a half note; that gets two clicks. As you get better at this exercise, gradually increase the tempo. When you've completed the exercise, play it starting on the first fret of the A string (which is a B♭ note) and repeat the pattern.

Ex. G. The Root–Five–Octave Exercise

The chromatic exercise and the root–five–octave exercise are enough of a technical foundation to establish our goals for this book. You can always play them faster *or* slower to make them more challenging. There are LOTS of other things you can do to develop your technique, and I suggest you continue to search out the information. But I said playing rock bass was easy, and I meant it. So… let's move on to learning about your fingerboard.

First Things First: Here's the Neck

The key to this method, and to bass playing in general, is knowing your fingerboard. The notes on the neck may seem like a lot to remember at first, but if you look closely, you'll see that it's all laid out very simply. To begin with, here is a grid of every note you have on the neck from the nut to the twelfth fret. The note on the twelfth fret (marked with double dots) is the same note as the open string, just an octave higher. Once you're above the 12th fret, all the notes repeat in the same order of appearance.

Notice that the note names follow the alphabet from A to G. In between most notes there is an *accidental*, a sharp or flat note. The exceptions are between E and F, and between B and C. Each accidental note can be called by two names, either a sharp or a flat (notated with ♯ and ♭, respectively). Which name you use depends on a few things—for now, it's just important that you recognize that they are the same note, so learn both of them.

Fig. 1. Fretboard Diagram

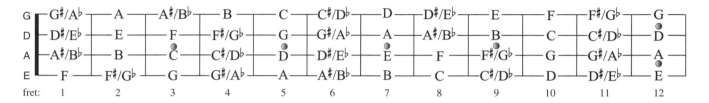

Since you'll be looking at written notation, let's get familiar with the notes on the fingerboard. Don't freak out! Reading notation is actually very simple, once you make the connection between what you're looking at and its location on the neck. As you'll see, most of these notes show up in more than one place on the fingerboard. You will soon learn the secret to figuring this out, but for now, refer to the fretboard diagram when locating the notes in the next few examples.

Bass players read music written in *bass clef,* also called the "F clef." The name indicates that the two dots in the clef symbol surround the line where the F note is written. The notes are written on a five-line grid called the *staff*. The notes get higher in pitch and move up the alphabet as you move up to higher lines and spaces on the staff.

Fig. 2

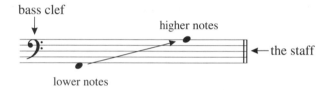

Here are the notes on the E string from open E to the fifth-fret A. Except for the A, each of these notes in this range occurs in only one place on a four-string bass. The A on the fifth fret is also the same written note as the open A string.

Ex. 1

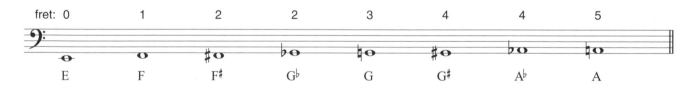

Here are the notes that occur on the first five frets of the A string. The D on the fifth fret is the same written note as the open D string. You will also find all these same notes located on the E string from the fifth fret to the tenth fret. We'll look at how that works in a minute.

Ex. 2

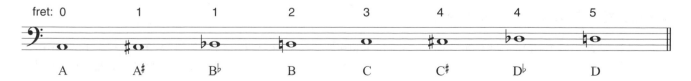

Here are the notes on the first five frets of the D string. They can also be found on the A string, from the fifth fret to the tenth fret. The open D at fret 0 is also the same D that shows up at the tenth fret on the E string. The D#/Eb is on the eleventh fret, and the E is the twelfth fret on the E string. The F, F#/Gb, and G can be found by continuing up the E string past the twelfth fret. You may not use these locations often, but they do pack a lot of punch when you need it.

Ex. 3

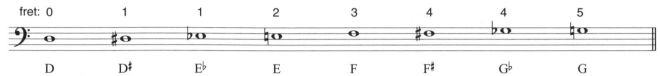

Now for the notes on the first five frets of the G string. If you've figured out the pattern, you already know that these notes also occur on the D string from the fifth fret to the tenth fret. They can also be found on the A string from the tenth fret to the fifteenth fret, and they also show up on the E string from the fifteenth fret to the twentieth fret. As I mentioned, the higher positions on the E string have a lot of bass energy behind them, so use them wisely!

Ex. 4

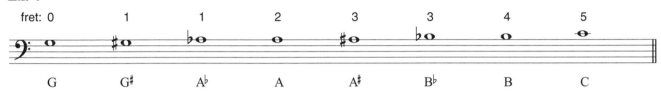

THE "SAME NOTE" PATTERN

Let's take a closer look at how the same note shows up in more than one place on the neck. Understanding this is one of the keys to fingerboard mastery. Let's use the A on the top line of the staff:

Ex. 5

This note is commonly played on the second fret of the G string. But, if you go down one string ("down" meaning to a lower-pitched string) and count up 5 frets ("up" meaning toward the higher notes), you'll find the exact same note. If you repeated this pattern from the A on the seventh fret, D string, you'd find the same note on the twelfth fret, A string. This "one string down, five frets up" pattern works all over the fingerboard for any note.

Fig. 3

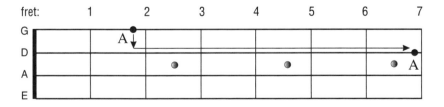

Once you understand this pattern on the neck, your life as a bass player becomes much simpler. Remember, except for the first four frets on your E string, EVERY note on the bass can be found in at least two locations. Make it a point to practice everything with this in mind—you'll be glad you did.

THE OCTAVE SHAPE

The next important fingerboard pattern to learn is the *octave* shape. "Octave" refers to the number eight. To find an octave, play a note (which becomes your root, or 1), count up eight notes along the major scale (do–re–mi–fa–sol–la–ti–do), and you'll wind up at the same note you started with (do)—only it's an octave higher. The root–octave pattern is used often in all styles of bass playing. It allows you to create the feeling of movement, and still only play the root note.

The octave shape on the fingerboard is easily learned. Play a root anywhere on the E or A string, then count up two frets and up two strings. That note is one octave higher than the root. The two notes have the same letter name, but are separated by the other notes of the major scale. The root and the octave can be interchanged freely. As you learn more, you'll see how the different octaves affect the feel of the music. The lower notes create more of a foundation, while the octaves can create a feeling of "lift" in a groove.

Here's the note G on the third fret of the E string, and its octave (with the major-scale notes in between):

Ex. 6

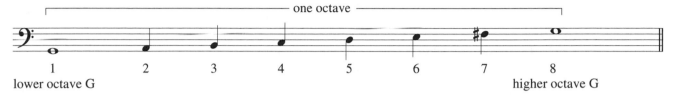

Here is how the shape looks on the fingerboard. Play the root with the first finger and the octave with the fourth finger (this reduces strain in the hand).

Fig. 4

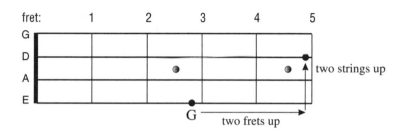

This shape will always produce an octave on the bass (assuming it's tuned properly!). But just to make things interesting: Remember how you can find notes in more than one place? Well, this particular higher octave G can be found in three other locations. The key to finding them is the "same note pattern" we talked about (Fig. 3, on page 16). Use the pattern going up and down from the fifth fret on the D string, and you'll find the same note is the open G, the tenth fret of the A string, and the fifteenth fret of the E string. On the staff, the note is written on the same space (as in Ex. 6), but you can play it in any of these three locations. Which one should you use? The answer depends mostly on which note you play before it, and which note you play after it. A general rule to follow is this: make your fingering as easy as possible—if it lays well, it plays well.

The Major Scale and Numerical System

The next important piece of business to learn is the major scale and its corresponding numerical system. Musicians of all types use this system to describe music. Melodies, bass lines, chord structures, chord progressions, modulations, and more can be described with the number system. We've already seen how the octave is eight notes up the major scale from the root. We use the same system to identify every other note in the scale.

Example 7 is the C major scale. Every note is numbered 1 through 8. I've also included the solfege syllables (do, re, mi, etc.) as they are familiar to anyone who's ever had to sit through *The Sound of Music*. These syllables are used worldwide in reference to the major scale. I've also included a simple "universal" fingering for the scale. This fingering gives you a major scale starting from any note on the E or A string, from the second fret or higher. (We'll talk about the exceptions soon.)

Ex. 7. C major scale

scale #:	1	2	3	4	5	6	7	8
	do	re	mi	fa	sol	la	ti	do
finger:	2	4	1	2	4	1	3	4

Let's see how the scale maps out on the fingerboard grid. Starting on the E or A string, put your second finger on the root and follow the fingering. The scale numbers will conveniently fall under the same fingers in any key. Very simple!

Fig. 5

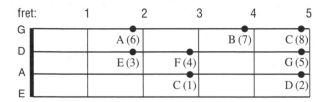

Because this fingering pattern is universal to all keys, and almost the entire fingerboard, it serves as a handy reference map for the numerical system. If you put your second finger on the root and follow the fingering, the rest of the numbers will conveniently fall under the same fingers in any key. Very simple!

Practice these two numerical sequences to get familiar with this system, and its grid pattern. Start in the key of C, and reference Figure 5 to make sure your fingers are in the right spot. To move to a new key, start on any note on the E or A string, above the second fret. Play the scale in the new key and figure out the names of the notes (refer back to Fig. 1, page 15, whenever needed). Then play the sequences in that key. Pay attention to:

1. the fingering
2. the scale numbers
3. the note names

If you can keep track of all three, you'll be in good shape.

The following sequence has you playing all the intervals contained within the major scale. The distance from 1 to 2 is called a 2nd; the distance from 1 to 3 is called a 3rd; from 1 to 4 is a 4th; 1 to 5 is a 5th; 1 to 6 is a 6th; 1 to 7 is a 7th; and 1 to 8 is an octave. Play these slowly and listen to the sounds they create. Being able to recognize these intervals by ear is very helpful.

Numerical Sequence #1

1 – 2 – 1 – 3 – 1 – 4 – 1 – 5 – 1 – 6 – 1 – 7 – 1 – 8 – 8 – 1 – 7 – 1 – 6 – 1 – 5 – 1 – 4 – 3 – 1 – 2 – 1 – 1

This next sequence is a very common chord progression; it may sound familiar to you. It shows up frequently in jazz, swing, and pop music of an older vintage. Again, start in the key of C and check yourself against the grid in Figure 5. Make sure you can recognize all the notes in this sequence by their names as well as their numbers. Pick other keys to work on; you have a total of 12 keys to choose from, but for starters, use the most common ones like G, D, A, E, F, and B♭. The other keys are less common, but eventually you'll need to know them all.

Numerical Sequence #2

1 – 6 – 2 – 5 – 3 – 6 – 2 – 5 – 1 – 3 – 4 – 2 – 3 – 6 – 2 – 5 – 1

Hey, remember how I said notes can be found in more than one location? Well, that's true for these sequences too. They won't fall under the fingers as naturally as they do when you stay in the major scale position, but just for a fun challenge, look for them in another location on the neck. I guarantee you'll learn something new and useful.

THE OPEN STRING POSITIONS

As I mentioned before, there are some exceptions to the universal major scale position. They are different because they use the open strings. Starting a major scale on the open E string makes the universal fingering impossible, yet we use the open E string all the time. You'll *need* to figure out THIS position! Here is a fingerboard grid of the E major scale in the open E position.

Fig. 6

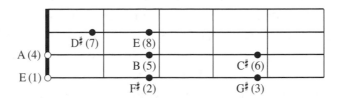

Here is how this scale looks written out on the staff. I've included the fingerings and solfege syllables too.

Ex. 8. E major scale—open position

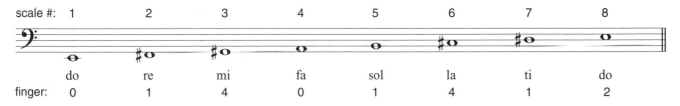

The open E position also works for an A major scale starting on the open A string; the fingering and numeric placement of the notes are exactly the same.

Now let's look at the other open-string position: for the F major scale, starting on the first fret of the E string. This scale uses the open A for the 3rd note, and the open D for the 6th. This position also works for a B♭ major scale starting on the first fret of the A string.

Fig. 7

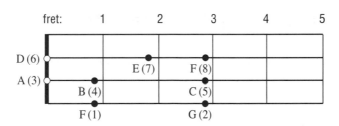

Here is the F major scale written out on the staff. Notice how the fingering uses the 1–2–4 fingering, with the first and fourth fingers for the whole steps between F and G, and B♭ and C. This reduces strain in the hand. Never force the hand open, or you're asking for problems down the road.

Ex. 9. F major scale

scale #:	1	2	3	4	5	6	7	8
	do	re	mi	fa	sol	la	ti	do
finger:	1	4	0	1	4	0	2	4

Once you get comfortable with the open string positions, go back to the numerical sequences and play them in the keys of E and F. While you're at it, play them in A and B♭ in open position as well. Get comfortable in open position; you'll spend a lot of time there.

The Basic Rhythms

Before we can move on, you'll need to learn some basic rhythms. Example 10 illustrates the most common rhythms used in this book. There are many other rhythms to learn, but we're going to keep it simple. The first rhythm (A) is the *whole note;* it gets four beats in standard 4/4 time. The second measure (B) shows *half notes,* which, as we've seen already, get two beats each. (C) is four *quarter notes;* each receives one beat (as we've seen in Ex. G). The *eighth note* (D) is worth half a beat; there are two eighths per quarter note. The counting pattern for eighth notes is: "one–and, two–and, three–and, four–and." The numbers are the *downbeats* and the "ands" are the *upbeats* (or sometimes called offbeats).

Dotted rhythms might seem a little tricky, but they are easy to get used to. You've heard them before; it's just a matter of learning to recognize the picture that goes with the sound. (E) starts with a *dotted quarter note*. The dot equals one half of whatever rhythm you put it next to, so a dotted quarter note equals one and a half quarter notes—or, simply, the duration of three eighth notes. The count for this rhythm is "one–and–two." The dotted quarter note is shown paired with an eighth note—one of the most popular rhythms in music.

Ex. 10

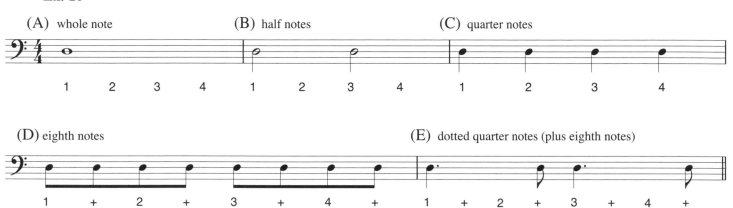

Take a Little Rest

Example 11 shows you the *rests* that correspond with the rhythms shown in Example 10. You don't play a rest, but you do have to count it. The rest acts as a placemarker in a measure of music, taking up the same amount of space as the rhythm it corresponds to. If you don't give the rests their full count, the feel of the music gets messed up. Honor your rests!

Ex. 11

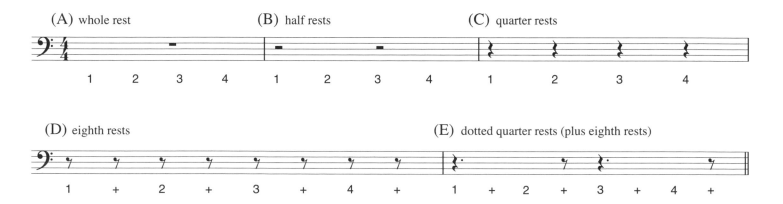

Study these rhythms and rests carefully. in Part 2 we'll start using them to create simple bass lines.

PART 2
Play the Root

Now that you have some basic "how-to" stuff under your fingers, let's get down to actually playing some bass lines. The most important concept of bass playing is to play the root of the chord. It's simple: when you see a chord symbol, or someone tells you a chord name, the root is the same as the letter name. For example: the chords E7, E minor 7th, E major 7th, E diminished 7th, E augmented major 7th, and E minor (major 7th)—all have the same root—E! It's up to you to decide which E you need to play. From your exploration of the fingerboard, you've discovered that you have at least seven E notes (more if you have over twenty frets, or a five- or six-string bass). Each E has its own particular function and flavor. For simplicity's sake, let's stick to the LOW ones; after all, you're a bass player and that's what we do—play low notes. Let's examine how to put this idea into action.

Before you play, you should always tune up. If you have a tuner, great—use it now. If not, here are the open strings to tune up with.

TUNING NOTES: G–D–A–E

Here's a very simple chord progression. Coincidentally, it uses three chords whose root notes are open strings. Be sure to mute the open D and A strings as you move back down to the E string. Notice that under each note is the letter R, which stands for Root. The root is the same as "1" in the numerical system you learned earlier; they are interchangeable. From now on, you'll see the numbers (and other markers, as they're introduced) under the notes. This will help you learn how the line is functioning, which makes it easier to find the notes in other places on the fingerboard. We'll learn to play this example with three different rhythms. First, solid quarter notes:

It's amazing how something so simple can sound so cool, isn't it? Get into the habit of finding new locations to play the same note. Check out the following fingerboard grid, and play the last example using some of the new note locations shown.

Grid 1

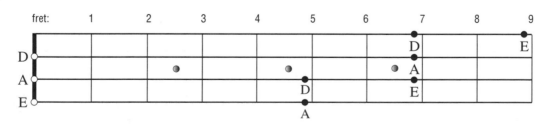

Now that you've experimented with different note placements, let's learn this example with other rhythms. First, we'll use the dotted quarter/eighth-note rhythm. Notice that it has a distinctly different feel from the first example. Also notice that the kick drum part matches the bass line. This is a very common approach in the rhythm section (bass and drums) for all kinds of music. The kick drum is one of the most important things to listen to when deciding what rhythm to choose for your own lines. While you're listening to the differences, also pay attention to how the guitar part has changed; the whole progression has a totally different feel.

The next rhythm is the classic "pumping eighth-note" feel. This is a great way to make a tune move. Pay close attention to the consistency of your eighth notes—make sure they are rhythmically accurate, consistent in volume and tone. Again, notice how the drum and guitar parts have changed to match the bass line. These decisions are made during band rehearsals, so you need to be prepared to change your part to accomodate the melody and feel of a tune—after all, we are there mainly to *support* the music.

Here's another progression to practice; it's 1–6–4–5 using the numerical system. Once again, we're only playing root notes. I've started with the low G on the third fret of the E string—it's the only location for that particular G. The next note is the open E string. The most logical place to play C is the third fret of the A string. D can be played either as open D, or on the fifth fret of the A string.

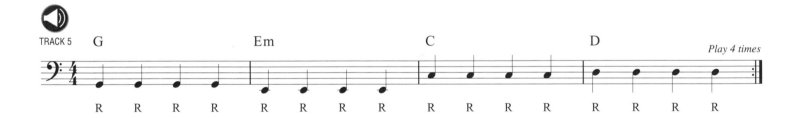

Did you notice that the second chord is an Em (minor) chord? Even if you don't know what that means—play E, and you're all set. Before we use the other rhythms, let's check out the fingerboard grid and see where else these notes can be found.

Grid 2

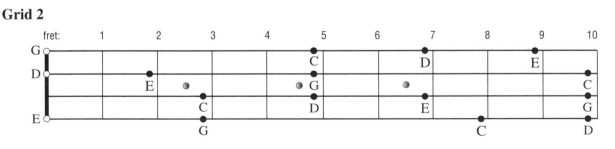

The grid goes up to the tenth fret, where you can find D on the E string and G on the A string. There are several places to find the roots of this chord progression; get familiar with many different ways to put them together. Look for ways to play them close to each other, although it is also common in rock bass to slide all over the neck—you can play this entirely on the E string if you want to. It's kind of cool to slide into your notes sometimes, and the C and D notes on the E string carry a lot of weight. There is no "wrong" way to do it—as long as you're playing the correct root—but keep in mind that the line has more integrity if you don't make huge jumps in register. For example: open G to open E, to fifth-fret C on the G string, to open D. That combination jumps register three times and sounds too choppy. Get the picture?

To try out the next rhythm, let's go back to the first set of note choices with a variation on the dotted quarter/eighth-note pattern. This time, make it a quarter note with an eighth rest on beats 2 and 4, and play an eighth-note "pickup" to beat 3 and beat 1 of the next measure. Leaving those beats open for the snare drum to hit by itself is a great way to tighten up the feel. It's one subtle way we can affect the groove.

Did you notice how the drums and guitar sound different from the previous track? There are many styles that can be called "rock," and many ways to play within any given style. You will need to be able to play your bass lines with several approaches. By listening to the music, you will learn to instinctively play the right groove.

This time, it's back to pumpin' eighth notes. Hey, it beats pumpin' gas!

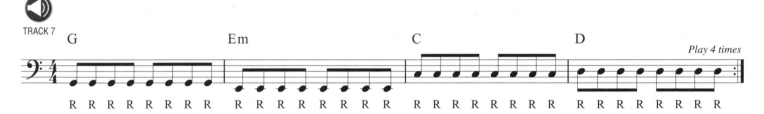

Now it's your turn to do your own thing. Here's a new progression, but there's no specific line written. You won't be reading bass lines most of the time, so get used to making your own choices. Take this example and run it through the same process: find the roots all over the neck, look for configurations that lay well together without skipping register, and play it with different rhythms.

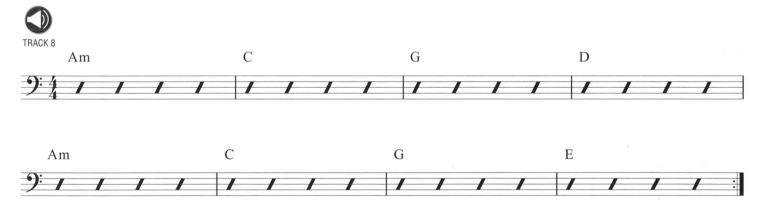

Using the Octave

Octaves are wonderful things. They allow you to create movement on a chord and still play just the root. As you've already learned, the octave is the same note as the root—just eight notes up the major scale—so you can always use it. Switching octaves gives the bass line a lift; you can definitely hear and feel the movement. Octaves are also a good way to switch to a higher register on the neck. Perhaps the most famous use of octaves in rock is "My Sharona" by The Knack. And, of course, there is 90 percent of everything recorded during the disco era...

Here's a line that uses the root and octave to create movement while on a chord.

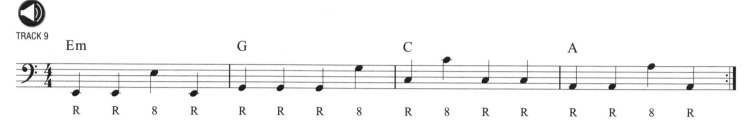

Now let's play this progression using the octave to jump registers.

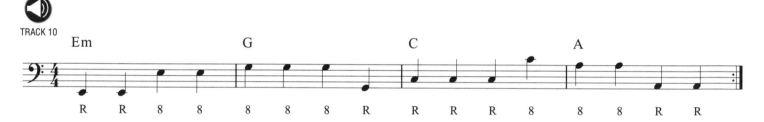

It's a subtle difference, but you can hear how the octave is used for different purposes. In bass playing, the fine details make it happen.

Now let's use the octave with some other rhythms. First, we'll use the dotted quarter/eighth-note rhythm. I'll mix up the function so we'll have movement within a chord, and register changes. I'll also add another four bars to the previous progression to give us more room to work with.

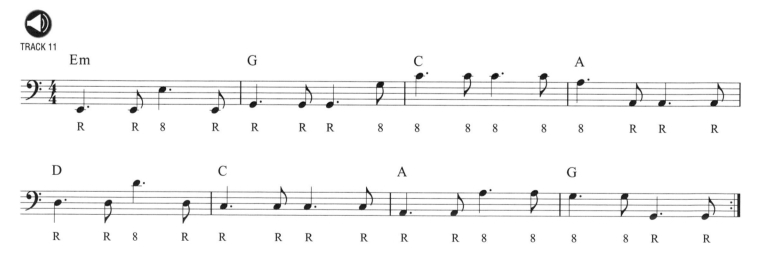

Notice that in some measures I didn't use the octave at all. Just because you *can* use it, doesn't mean you *have* to use it.

Now here's the eighth-note version. With this rhythm, the octave acts as a nice accent to the beat. It can be used to switch registers too. Again, notice that there are measures where you stay on the root.

TRACK 12

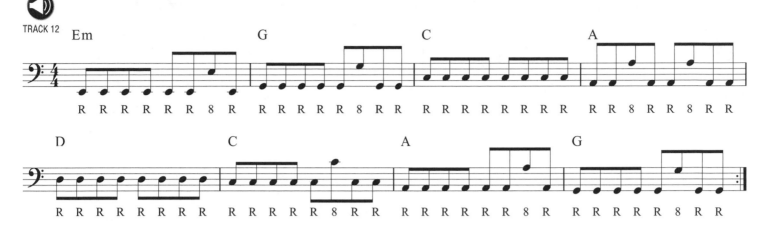

For more practice, you can go back to Tracks 2–8 and play them using the root and octaves. You can also jump ahead to the end of the book and play through the full-length tunes using what you know so far. It may not seem like much to work with, but you'd be surprised how much can be done with such simple tools.

Adding the Fifth

The next note choice we'll learn to use is the *5th*. The 5th (or "5") is a very important note in bass playing; it creates a strong gravitational pull back to the root. This pull is something we bassists use in everything we play. As an experiment, play a major scale—any key will do. Play it a few times up and down to establish the sound of the key in your head. Now, play from the root to the 5th and stop. It sort of hangs there, doesn't it? Play it again, up to the 5th, let it hang for a little bit, and then play the root. When you hit the root, it feels like "home." Improper placement of the 5th in a bass line can create a lop-sided, backwards feel. There may be a time for that, but for now, let's learn how to use the 5th the way it works best.

There are a few patterns on the neck that will produce the root–5. We'll focus first on the most logical one. Most of the notes on the bass (except for the first four frets on the E string) will have an *upper 5* and a *lower 5*. The upper and lower 5 are the same note name, but in different octaves. Grid 3 shows you how that works.

For example, the third fret on the A string is a C. The upper 5 is two frets up (fifth fret) and one string up (the D string); that note is a G. The lower 5 is on the same fret (fret 3) but one string lower (the E string). That note is also G, but in a lower octave. You can use either the upper or lower 5th, but they have a different feel, so listen to how they work and make your choice based on knowing the difference. The root (C) can also be played on the E string, eighth fret, in which case the upper 5 is still G, found two frets up and one string up at the tenth fret, A string. to play the lower 5, you would have to jump all the way down to the third fret on the E string.

Grid 3

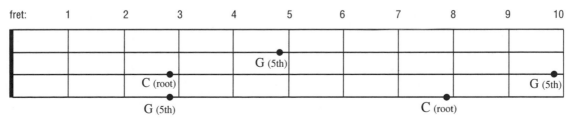

Here's an example using the 5th. I've cut the rhythm back to simple half notes, which get two counts each. This is a very common approach to playing many styles of music; root–5 in half notes works for rock, jazz, Latin, country (especially country!), and more. It's very simple, and proper placement of the 5th makes it work.

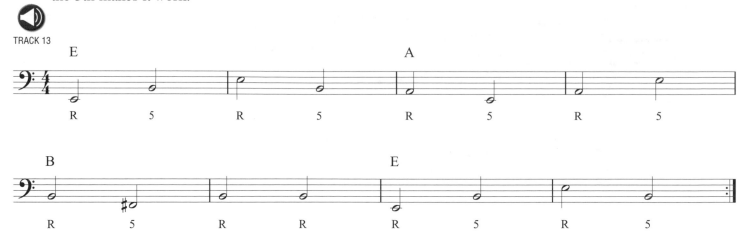

TRACK 13

Here's a grid to show you the many locations for these note choices. Notice that some of these notes belong to more than one chord. For example, E is obviously the root of the E chord, but it's also the 5th of the A chord. B is the root of the B chord, but also the 5th of the E chord. Look over these alternate locations and see how many ways you can play Examples 13–15.

Grid 4

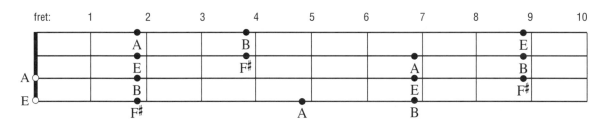

This example uses the same progression with the quarter/eighth-note pickup rhythm. Notice how sometimes the 5th is used as a quarter, and sometimes it's the eighth note.

TRACK 14

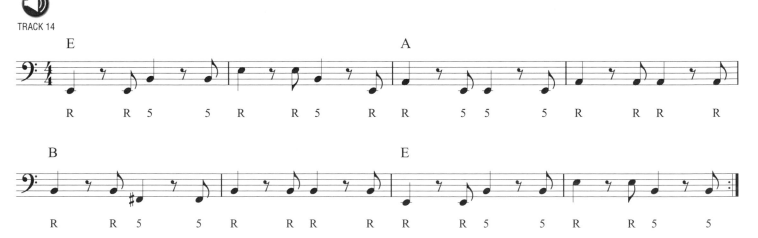

Now let's use the 5th in a line that pumps eighth notes. Notice that the 5 gets used to add little accents to the line, and as a "bridge" to the octave. Now you see how the *Root–5–8* exercise you practiced comes in handy. It's a classic way to create movement in a bass line without getting specific about major, minor, or different types of 7th chords. They are "safe" choices for any type of chord, with only a few rare exceptions. The shape falls naturally under the fingers, and it sounds good. You'll be using R–5–8 patterns for the rest of your bass playing life

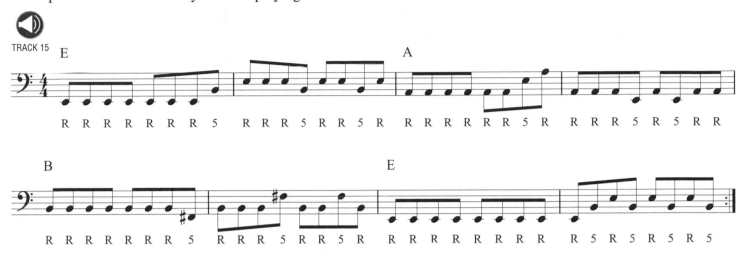

Now it's your turn to put the R–5–8 into action. Here's a new progression to practice. First, find all the roots in as many locations as possible on the neck. Then find the lower and upper 5th for each root. Play the example with half notes, dotted quarter/eighth notes, and straight eighth-note rhythms. Experiment with different ways to order the notes. Go back to the previous examples and play them with R–5–8, then move ahead to the other examples, and use them for more practice.

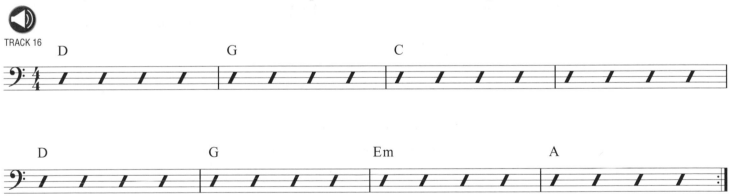

Approach Notes

Now that you have some experience with the root–5–8 shape, let's look at ways to create more movement in the bass line. Although thousands of hit records feature the bass playing "just" the root, there are things we can add to our bass lines to create a greater sense of *destiny*—when you can feel where the line is going. Creating moments like that in a bass line can make a song really happen.

Approach notes can be used to create movement during a chord, or as a way to get from one chord to the other. The approach note precedes the *target note*—usually the root of the next chord, or the 5th of the chord you're currently playing. There are three types of approach notes we'll learn: the chromatic approach, the scale approach, and the dominant approach. Each works in its own unique way to create movement over a chord, or take you to the next chord.

CHROMATIC APPROACH

Chromatic approach is the easiest type of approach note to grasp; it's simply a half step away from your target note. By now, we all know that a half step is one fret on the bass (we DO know this—right?). For example, a chromatic approach to a G would be either F♯/G♭ or A♭/G♯. (Notice how I mentioned both names for the chromatic notes; they can be called by either one depending on the context.) You can find a G in many places on the fingerboard, and you can also find its corresponding chromatic approach notes in several places as well. It's easy to figure them out, because they are always one fret above or below the target. If you know the location of G, you automatically know where F♯/G♭ is (one fret lower) and where A♭/G♯ is (one fret higher). The only exception is the open G string; its lower chromatic approach note is found on the fourth fret of the D string, which also acts as the lower chromatic approach note for the G on the 5th fret of the D string. By now, the patterns on the neck have become clear to you, and you recognize that open G and fifth-fret D-string G are the same note. Take a look at Grid 5 to see what we've just been talking about.

Grid 5

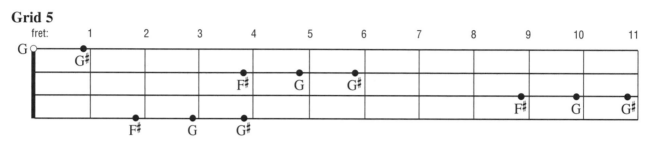

Tracks 17 and 18 use chromatic approach. On some chords, we use a chromatic note to approach the 5—this creates movement within the chord. We'll also use it to move toward the next chord change—giving the bass line a little "destiny." The chromatic approach notes are marked with the letters "Chr."

Grid 6 shows you the target notes (roots and 5ths) for Tracks 17 and 18. The chromatic approaches are one fret (a half step) above or below these targets.

Grid 6

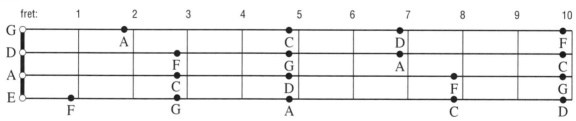

TRACK 17

Now let's use the same progression with an eighth-note feel.

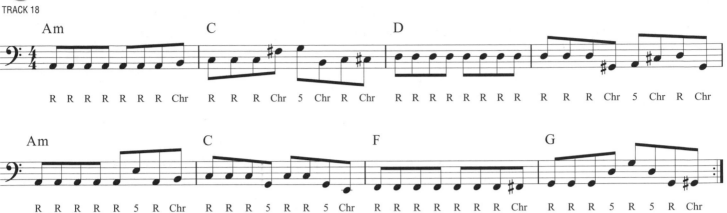

Now it's your turn. Here's a new progression. Find the roots in all locations, then the 5ths. The locations of the chromatic approaches should be obvious to you by now. Play the example using different rhythms.

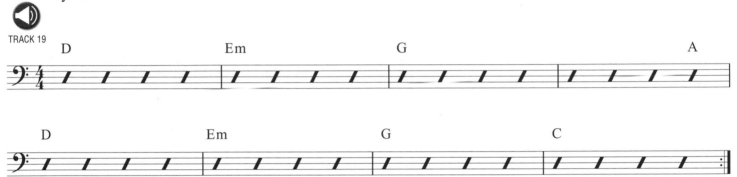

SCALE APPROACH

The next approach technique we'll learn is *scale approach*. Scale approach uses the next closest *scale tone* on either side of the target note. Most often, that means using a whole step (two frets) to approach our target—of course, there are also half steps in scales, and in some cases a scale approach note may be a half step (chromatic). For now, it doesn't matter what you call it—just use it if it sounds good. Scale approach creates a nice melodic sound, though it can be tricky to use because there are different types of scales, and the same type of chord may take a different scale depending on what chords are surrounding it. Rather than get too involved in a theory discussion, we'll assume that it's going to be a whole step most of the time; if it sounds wrong, make it a half step.

Grid 7 shows you scale approach notes for a G7 chord. The root is obviously G, and the 5th is D. The scale approaches for the root are A from above and F from below. The scale approaches for the 5 are E from above and C from below. Isn't it amazing how many choices you have for just one chord? Learn all the options—you'll have more to work with, you won't get stuck playing the same old thing, and each note location has its own unique texture. For example, the F on the third fret D string is the exact same pitch as the F on the eighth fret A string, yet they are very different in tonal quality and "bass energy." The eighth fret A-string note has much more power and "boom" factor; the third fret D location is a little sweeter and cleaner. Taking notice of these subtleties helps you become a more effective bass player.

Grid 7

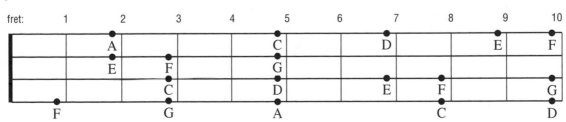

Let's look at an example of scale approach in a bass line. Grid 8 shows you the root and 5th locations for all the chords in this progression. Some of the notes have two purposes. For example, A is the root of Am, and it's also the 5th of Dm. F is the root of the F chord, and the 5th of the B♭ chord. D is the root of the Dm chord, and the 5th of the G chord. Learn all the locations for the notes, and then start playing the example. As always, look for as many different ways to play it as possible.

Grid 8

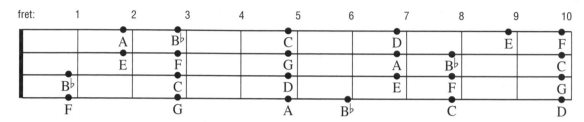

Looking at the written bass line, notice that in measure 6 we have a note marked 5/Sc. That note (C) has two functions: it's the 5th of the F chord, and it acts as a scale approach from below to the Dm chord. Also, in measure 8, the last note (G) is marked R/Sc because it's both the root of the G chord and a scale approach from below leading to the Am chord.

TRACK 20

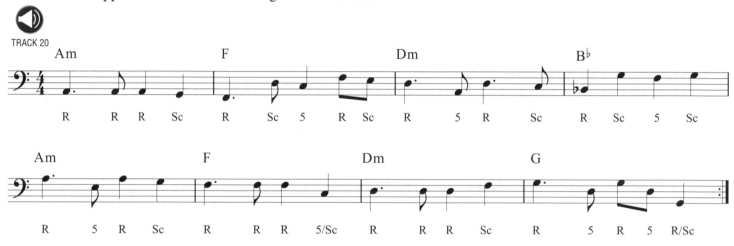

Here's the same progression using the eighth-note rhythm. It's definitely getting more active—maybe even a little *too* active! I'm using the idea alot for an eight-measure phrase, and while it doesn't hurt to play this much occasionally, remember to keep your lines balanced by just staying on the root sometimes.

TRACK 21

Here's a progression for you to figure out on your own. As always, find the roots and 5ths in as many locations as you can. Then locate the scale approach notes for each chord's root and 5th—most often this will be a whole step above or below the note. Remember that some choices sound better than others, so listen and decide according to your ears. Experiment with using the scale approach notes sparingly, then use them often. See how this affects the bass line. Then, try alternating between chromatic and scale approach. Create a bass line that uses the best of both choices.

TRACK 22

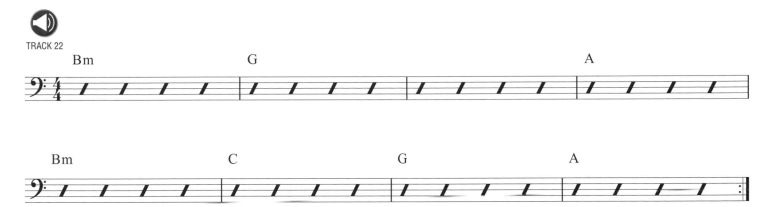

DOMINANT APPROACH

The last type of approach note we'll learn is the *dominant approach.* "Dominant" is another name for the 5th, so dominant approach uses the 5th of the target note as an approach note. Many times, a chord progression may have this built in. For example, when a song goes from Em to A7, E is the 5th of A. When you play the root of the Em chord going to the A7, you are automatically using dominant approach. This can also be called "dominant root motion." It's such a strong pattern that you'll see it show up everywhere.

The place where dominant approach creates something new and interesting is when the root motion *isn't* dominant. For example, if the first chord is Em and the second chord is G, using a D (the 5th of G) to approach the G chord is a cool and interesting choice. The other way we can use dominant approach is within the chord as an approach to the 5th. We use the 5 *of the* 5, which creates an interesting new sound in the measure. You already know how to find the 5th of any chord, and the 5 *of* 5 is really scale degree 2.

Here's an example of dominant approach in the bass line. When the root motion is already dominant, you won't notice it much, but I'll show you how to use it as an approach to the 5 (5 *of* 5). When the root motion isn't dominant, you'll see how effective this technique is. Grid 9 shows you the locations of all the roots, 5ths, and dominant approaches for the next progression.

Grid 9

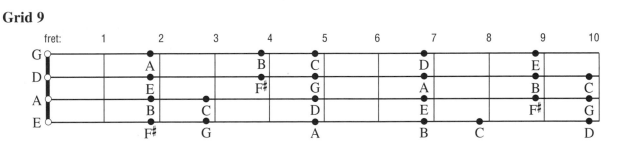

Now here's the progression using dominant approach:

TRACK 23

How about an eighth-note version?

TRACK 24

That last example gets pretty active. While it's good to know how to get busy with the bass line, it's also important to know *when* to get busy. Just remember: less is still more when it comes to laying down a solid groove. I've condensed a lot of ideas into this eight-measure phrase, but in the "real" world, you might use one fourth of this amount of material to create a line. When you have to stay out of a singer's way, you play less. When you have two guitars, keyboards, background singers, and a full horn section, you play MUCH less.

Here's a chance for you to put together your own line. Find the roots and 5ths all over the neck, and figure out the dominant approaches. For more practice, learn the chromatic and scale approaches for this example as well. In fact, go back and re-learn every single example we've played so far, and try the different approaches you didn't get to try the first time through. You'll learn a lot more that way.

TRACK 25

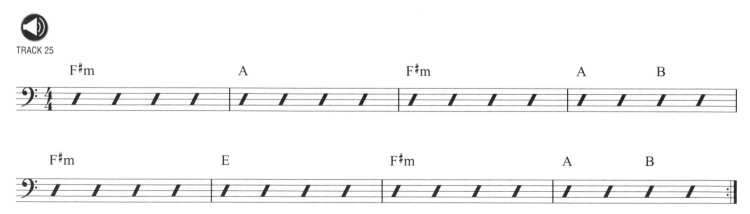

PART 3
Box Shapes, Pentatonic Scales, and Blues

Now that we've learned how to construct bass lines using the approach/target method, let's look at some of the other elements involved in playing rock bass. The *box shape* is a very common form on the bass. It's called a box because the note pattern forms a rectangular shape on the fingerboard. Using the first finger to play the root on the E string, the box includes scale numbers 4, 5, ♭7, and 8. If you continue up one more string, you also have ♭3 and 4.

Grid 10 shows you the layout of the basic box shape. This shape can be moved around the neck easily; the first finger on the E string becomes the root of the key. Grid 10 is the key of G, and the notes are labeled according to their scale numbers—but by now you should know the names of each note shown.

Grid 10

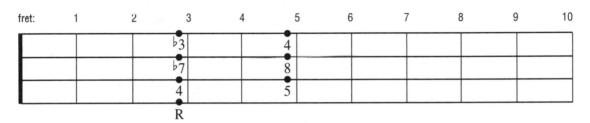

The box shape is virtually identical to something known as the *minor pentatonic scale*. In fact, there is only one note missing—the minor pentatonic scale adds a ♭3 on the same string as the root. The complete scale only goes to the octave, but staying in the position, you can also catch the ♭3 and 4 on the G string, just like in the previous example. Grid 11 shows the G minor pentatonic scale.

Grid 11

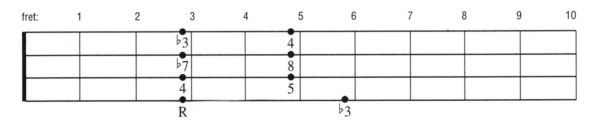

These two very similar fingerboard patterns are the source of a lot of ideas used in rock bass lines. Let's look at a classic box-shape line that's incredibly simple, and gets played all the time. Grid 12 shows you the layout. The line is R–8–♭7–5, and for this example it's in the key of G.

Grid 12. I–G7 chord

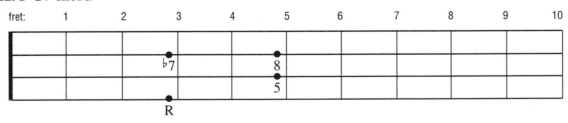

Here is the line written out:

Ex. 12

33

Now we'll take this basic box-shape line and create a blues form out of it. The *12-bar blues* is one of the most common song forms in rock, jazz, blues (of course), country, R&B, and popular music in general. As a style of music, the blues is truly the foundation of rock as we know it. Blues legend and rock pioneer Muddy Waters wrote a song called "The Blues Had a Baby, and They Called It Rock 'n' Roll"—truer words were never spoken. During the post-WWII era, the early blues masters in Chicago were the first to use electric instruments to play what was originally an acoustic folk-style blues that originated in the Mississippi Delta region. The resulting music was more urban-sounding and much louder. It influenced all the early rock performers, most notably Chuck Berry, and in a sense BECAME rock 'n' roll. Even the British Invasion of the '60s was a product of the post-war blues style. If you look back at bands like the Beatles, The Rolling Stones, Jethro Tull, Fleetwood Mac, Led Zeppelin, and many others, you'll see that their first albums featured mostly blues-oriented material. But enough history; let's look at "da blues."

The 12-bar blues follows a set format with a few possible variations. The simplest version (Track 26) has the I chord for four measures. In the fifth measure, you go to the IV chord for two bars. In measures 7 and 8, you return to the I chord. In measure 9 you have the V chord for one measure; measure 10 is the IV chord for one measure; and measures 11 and 12 go back to the I chord.

Since this box-shape line is only one measure long, we'll move it around the fingerboard according to the format you've just read. Staying in the key of G, here are the grids to show you where the IV (C) and V (D) chords lay on the neck. Please remember that you need to know the names of the notes you're playing; don't just think of them as shapes.

Grid 13. IV–C7 chord

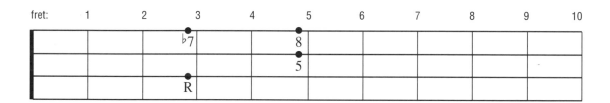

Grid 14. V–D7 chord

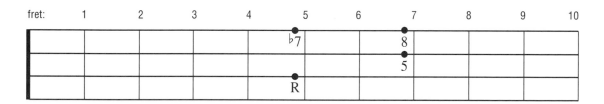

Here is the 12-bar box-shape blues line written out in G. This example has a "shuffle" feel (we'll get into that a little more later). You can play this line in any key by simply changing the starting location of your first finger and following the same pattern of notes. To play a blues in A, put your first finger on the fifth fret of the E string and play the pattern. For a blues in F, put your first finger on the first fret of the E string and follow the pattern. It's easy!

TRACK 26

Another cool way to play this example is using the *shuffle* or "double-stroke" rhythm. It might look a little scary, but listen to the recorded bass line. You already know what this sounds like; it's just a matter of getting the feel into your hands.

TRACK 27

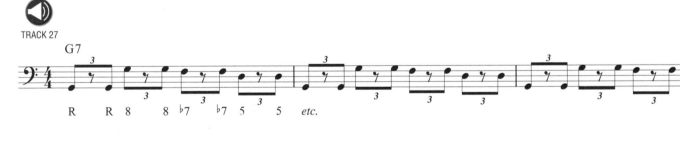

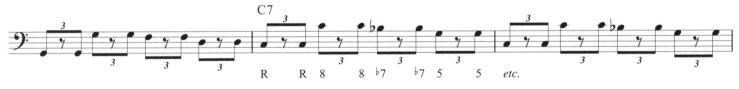

Here's another box-shape line. It's played with an even eighth-note feel, and has more of a rock 'n' roll groove. This groove works great for older R&B tunes like "Mustang Sally." This line is also in the key of G, and the note locations are the same as in the previous examples.

TRACK 28 G7

Example 13 shows you some variations of the box-shape line. They all use the same exact notes, but in different order, maybe with a slight change in the rhythm. You can substitute any of these patterns over Track 28. Simply use the new "lick" as the basis for the blues pattern—four times on the I chord, two times on the IV, and back to the I chord twice; then once on the V chord, once on the IV chord, and twice on the I chord. That's all there is to it.

Ex. 13

Now it's time for you to do a little thinking (but not too much). This next track is the same groove and bass line as the last one, except it's in the key of A. This means you have to figure out how to play it in a new key, with new note locations. It's VERY easy. In addition to moving the entire position and repeating the exact same pattern, you can make it more challenging by playing the A7 and E7 patterns in open position. You have open E and A strings (open D too—try that!). How would this line work using these options? It's totally possible, and the low E string sounds great. So your mission (should you choose to accept it) is to find more than one way to play this line in the key of A (there are several). Also, use the box-shape variations shown in Example 13.

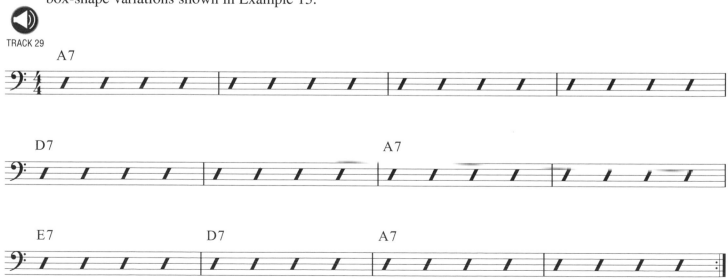

TRACK 29

THE WALKING BLUES LINE

As a rock bass player, you MUST know this classic line. It's been used for decades in swing, R&B, jazz, rock, country— everything! You'll recognize it instantly. This is the type of line that was played on early rock records of the 1950s, especially Chuck Berry's. When rock was first "invented," there was no such thing as a "rock musician." These early recordings were made by jazz, R&B, and blues players. This bass line is a hold-over from those styles, so it became the first rock 'n' roll bass line.

First, lets look at this line in a "universal fingering" key like A♭. Don't freak out about the key—if you learn the position, you can shift it anywhere on the neck and immediately play it in other keys. Of course, even in a "universal" key, there is more than one way to play it. The grids map out the locations of the notes, indicated by their scale numbers. There are at least three different ways to play this line, all of which lay well on the fingerboard, and each way is easily transposed to a new key by starting on the new root. Make sure you try the line several ways; you might break a string one day and be forced to find a different fingering!

TRACK 30

Here are the grids for the individual chords. Can you see the three different ways to play this line? Here's a hint: start on the root with your fourth finger, or with your second finger, or your first finger. The most common approach to this line is the one starting with the second finger, but the others are good to know.

Grid 15. A♭7

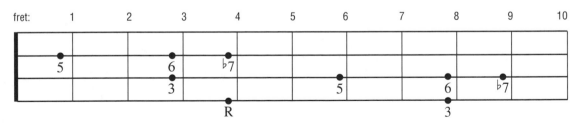

Grid 16. D♭7

Perhaps you've noticed that this bass line uses a two-measure repeating pattern. It goes up in the first measure, and down in the second. This works fine until you get to the last four measures, where there is only one measure of E♭7 and one measure of D♭7. We solve this easily by playing a one-measure pattern (R–3–5–3) for each of these chords. For the E♭7 chord, there are the same three options that we had with the A♭7 and D♭7 chords, starting on the fourth, second, or first fingers. However, there are two more options that are specific to this particular chord. First, you can use the E♭ on the first fret of the D string for the root, then play the open G as the 3rd, and the third-fret B♭ on the G string as the 5th. The second option substitutes the fifth-fret G on the D string as the 3rd.

Grid 17. E♭7

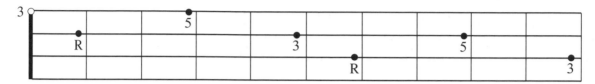

Another classic approach to this line is to play each note twice as eighth notes. It creates more rhythmic push and an aggressive feel.

TRACK 31

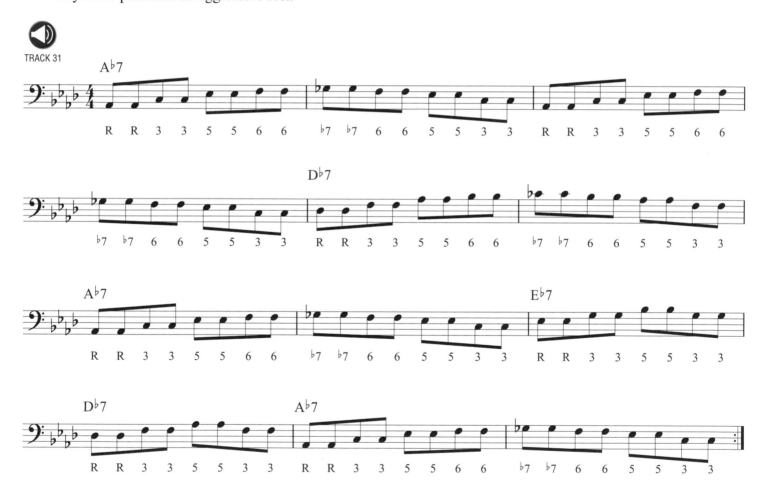

Okay, now it's time to put the awesome power of your brain to work. We've learned this bass line in A♭ using several shapes, but the most popular key in rock is undoubtedly E. Now it's time for you to figure out this bass line in E, all by yourself—no grids to show you where the notes are. If necessary, refresh your memory by looking back at the open E position grids, then figure out the line using the scale numbers. You can do it! It's easy. You'll be using open E and open A as your roots. The B is... well, you'll find it. Practice this line in both quarter- and eighth-note versions.

TRACK 32

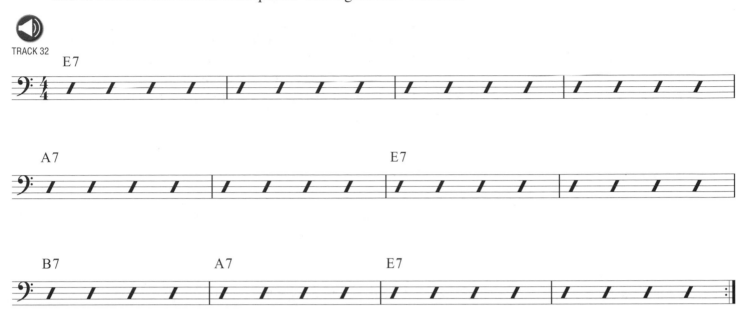

That wasn't too hard, was it? Although I've designed this book to be easy to use, it's important to stretch your mind and figure things out for yourself. Instead of using tablature to learn every example, you've become accustomed to looking for alternatives. As you know by now, learning more than one way to play a line gives you a real musical advantage. Rock bass playing is fairly simple, but understanding what you play opens up more options. You can learn new songs faster, create your own parts on the spot, and play a wider range of styles. It's not uncommon for bass players to be in several bands at once, or to become freelancers and play with anyone who calls them for a gig. To pull this off, you need to know your bass intimately, understand how to create lines, and *groove*. By now, you're well on your way to becoming a solid and aware bass player. Let's look ahead at some new ideas that will make your bass playing even more interesting.

New Rhythms

Up to this point in the book, the rhythms we've used have been fairly simple. You've worked with the dotted quarter/eighth-note feel, consistent pumping eighth notes, quarter-note walking lines, and a shuffle feel. There are many rhythmic variations in rock music, and while they may look scary when you see them written on paper, I guarantee that you can learn them immediately by listening. Your brain works amazingly fast when it comes to learning rhythms by ear. For this upcoming section, make sure you listen to the rhythms as I've played them on the audio—don't let the written music scare you off! First, we'll look at a new rhythm played on just the root, and then we'll see how the new rhythm can be used in a more active bass line.

ANTICIPATING THE DOWNBEAT

One of the most common rhythmic ideas in rock (and many other styles of music) is to *anticipate the downbeat*. We play on the "and" (+) of beat 4, and hold it through the *downbeat* (beat 1) of the next measure. This creates forward movement in the bass line and gives the music a nice edge.

anticipation

After hearing this a few times, I'm sure you can think of many tunes that do this. Let's look at a bass line that uses this rhythm over a chord progression. We'll keep the bass line simple—strictly roots and 5ths. When you get comfortable with this rhythm, feel free to add other elements like approach notes to the line. Notice how I anticipate the downbeat of measure 1 at the repeat sign—let this note sustain through the dotted quarter note that begins the pattern again.

TRACK 34

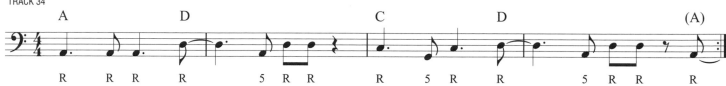

Let's look at some more rhythms that anticipate the downbeat. This next one is a little more active within the measure, and the steady eighth notes for beats 3 and 4 of measure 2 provide a great place to add approach notes.

TRACK 35

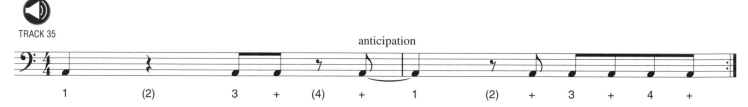

anticipation

Now let's see this rhythm used over a chord progression. Notice that I'm using scale approach notes to add more interest. Also, I've anticipated the downbeat of measure 1 on the repeat, by playing the root (octave) on the "and" of beat 4 in the last measure. This is not a rhythmic hold, however; it's a *melodic anticipation*.

TRACK 36

Here's another rhythm that anticipates the downbeat. Pumping straight eighth notes with an anticipation is a classic approach. In measure 4, we see a G used to approach the low E that anticipates the downbeat of measure 1. This note is listed as a scale approach, because it's from the E minor pentatonic scale.

TRACK 37

UPBEATS

Another rhythmic approach that's common is using the *upbeats*, or "ands" (+) of a measure to create a bass line. This rhythm gives your bass line a cool, bouncy feel. First, let's look at just the rhythm to get used to it. It's important to balance this out with some downbeats; after all, we want the groove to "settle in" too.

TRACK 38

Here's another line that uses the upbeat rhythm. In measure 2, we have a double chromatic approach up to the G in measure 3. Measure 3 is a box-shape line.

TRACK 39

SIXTEENTHS

Sixteenth-note rhythms may be scary looking, but rest assured—you've heard them all before. The tricky part is that the measure gets subdivided into sixteen equal parts; each quarter note is divided into four sixteenth notes. The most common way to count sixteenths is using the syllables *one-e-and-a*, *two-e-and-a*, and so on.

Below you'll find a measure of sixteenths with the count underneath. Listen to the example to hear how the quarter note gets broken up into four equal parts. Practice playing straight sixteenths at slow and medium tempos. Use the metronome on quarter notes, and make sure you nail the downbeats. Sixteenth-note feels are very common in rock, funk, Latin, and many other styles of music. Getting comfortable with this level of rhythmic activity is important. Don't rush it!

TRACK 40

Play 4 times

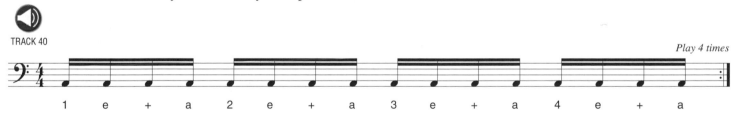

Sixteenth-note rhythms are simple to hear, and once you get used to breaking up the quarter note into four parts, they are not at all difficult to read. Here are some sixteenth-note rhythms that frequently show up in rock bass playing.

This line uses primarily the roots, and leaves a lot of space. Get used to following the counting pattern underneath the line.

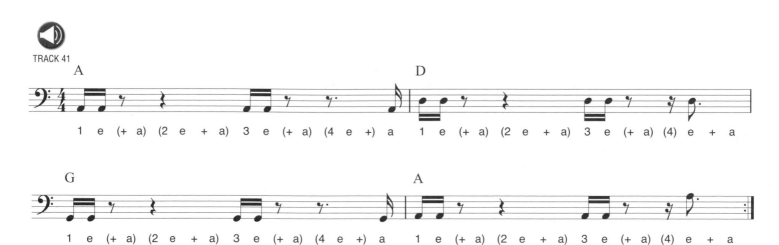

1 e (+ a) (2 e + a) 3 e (+ a) (4 e +) a   1 e (+ a) (2 e + a) 3 e (+ a) (4) e + a

1 e (+ a) (2 e + a) 3 e (+ a) (4 e +) a   1 e (+ a) (2 e + a) 3 e (+ a) (4) e + a

Here's another sixteenth-note rhythm. An easy way to remember how it sounds is to assign the words "check on dat" to the notes.

"check   on   dat"   "check   on   dat"   *Play 4 times*

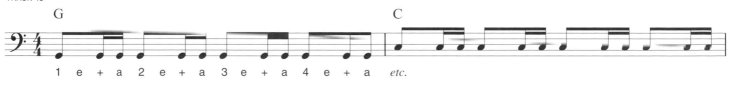

1   e   +   a   (2   e   +   a)   3   e   +   a   (4   e   +   a)

Here's a cool line that uses the same rhythm as its basis.

A   *Play 4 times*

1 e + a (2 e + a) 3 e + a (4 e + a)   1 e + a (2 e +) a 3 e + a 4 e + a

Here is a sixteenth-note rhythm that has a "galloping" feel.

                                                    Play 4 times

1   e   +   a   2   e   +   a   3   e   +   a   4   e   +   a

This line uses the "gallop" rhythm over a typical rock progression. Focus on keeping the notes consistent and driving. This line is a good candidate for pick-style playing.

G   C

1 e + a 2 e + a 3 e + a 4 e + a   *etc.*

B♭   F

Wrapping It Up

There are many other rhythms used in rock music, but the ones we've looked at are among the most common. To learn more rhythms, simply listen to music. When you hear a cool rhythm, pick it up by ear. Sing it until you can match the song, and transfer it to the bass. It's amazingly simple.

Up to this point, we've looked at a lot of information. It will still take some time before you have absorbed everything in this book and it becomes part of your musical being. The most important things to remember are:

- Play simply—there's more going on in a tune than just the bass line.

- Outline the root motion—it's the bottom line.

- Choose rhythmic material that works with the song, and MAKE IT GROOVE!

- Look for more than one way to play any bass line—different locations on the neck produce different tone qualities and new ideas, and give you a backup plan in case of broken strings.

- Use a metronome to develop solid time; practice playing things slowly before you try to shred.

- Listen to how you connect with the drummer—bass and drums are two sides of the same coin.

- Develop a consistent right hand—it's the heart of your sound.

- Play with authority, but be flexible enough to adapt to change.

- Don't let the lead singer bug you—they are a completely different animal.

Full-Length Tunes

Throughout this book, we've put the ideas learned into use with short four- and eight-measure mini-tunes. Now it's time to work with some bigger forms. The following tunes will have several different sections, and opportunities to try different rhythms. There will be no specific written bass lines—just the chord changes, and rhythmic suggestions. The goal is for you to put together your own bass line, just like you would if you were in a band or on a gig. Of course, you can also listen to my recorded bass line; you can even learn it by ear, write it down, whatever. But remember, learning to develop your own part is a crucial skill all bass players need to know. The truth is, most people have no idea what to tell you to play. It's up to you—you're the bass player!

TUNE #1

Here's a very cool but simple tune. Each section has a letter to identify it. The form is A–A–B–A–A–B–B, and it ends on an Am chord. The A section is a verse, and the B is called the chorus. The A section has a more laid-back feel, while the chorus drives harder. A typical approach might be to play whole notes for the very first A section, then do the dotted quarter/eighth-note rhythm for the second A section. The chorus can take a pumping eighth-note feel. Catch the anticipated downbeat to measure 4 of the B section.

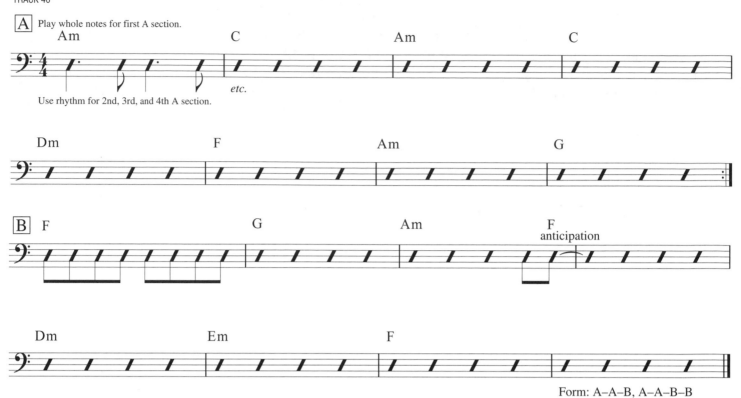

Form: A–A–B, A–A–B–B

TUNE #2

This three-part tune has a rootsy, Rolling Stones-ish feel. The A section has a mostly quarter-note feel, but it's mixed with some eighth notes and has a few anticipations (for the sake of clarity, they are marked "ant"). The B section goes to a straight eighth-note feel; you can use the walking blues line pattern from Track 32 (page 39) to give the section a "boogie" feel. The C section has a specific rhythm to use: just hit two eighth notes on beats 1 and 3, and catch the pumping eighth-note buildup back to the A section. The form of this one is A–B–A–B–C–A–B–B and ends on an anticipated E chord.

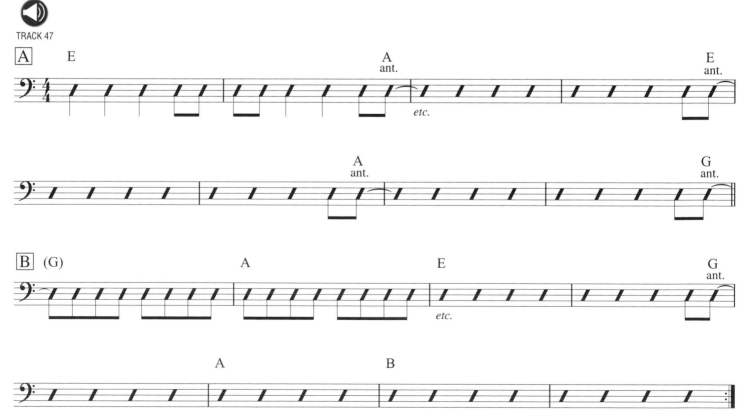

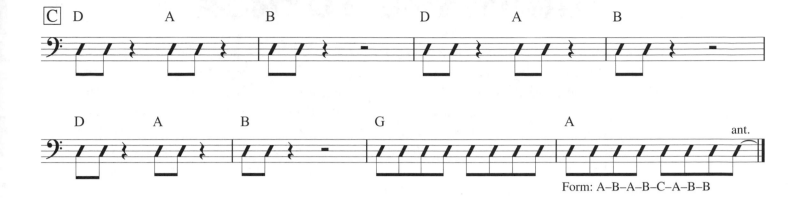

Form: A–B–A–B–C–A–B–B

TUNE #3

This tune also has three sections: A, B, and C. Listen to the rhythm of the drum and guitar parts to help you figure out the best way to play each section. The chords and rhythm of section C are perfect for trying out different approach types. Mix chromatic, scale, and dominant approaches to the roots—it's easy and effective.

TRACK 48

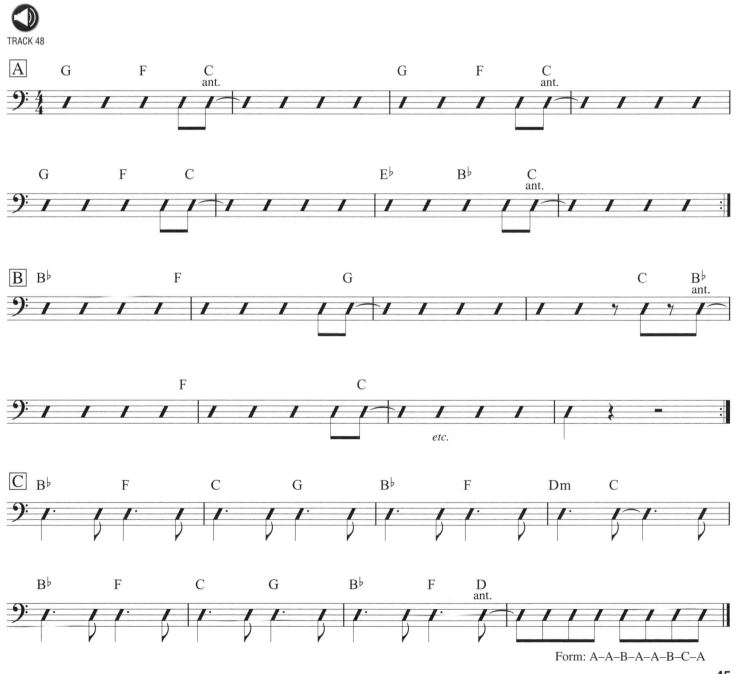

Form: A–A–B–A–A–B–C–A

ABOUT THE AUTHOR

Ed Friedland has become known as one of the world's leading bass teachers. Ed taught at Berklee College of Music, Boston College, and Arizona State University, as well as authored video courses for Scottsbasslessons.com, and Bass Guru. Through his writing for *Bass Player* magazine, many Hal Leonard instructional books and DVDs, and years of teaching, Ed has illuminated the art and craft of bass playing to countless "low-enders," both student and professional. More information about his other books and a discography can be found at *www.edfriedland.com*. For nine years, Ed produced bass demos on YouTube as "The Bass Whisperer." As a performer, he has played in many different situations encompassing rock, blues, jazz, fusion, funk, R&B, country, Latin, classical, theater, and various ethnic styles—all of which prepared him well to hold down the bottom for the Grammy Award winning band, The Mavericks. A New York City native, Ed has toured the world with the Mavericks, performing at festivals, on radio, and television.

BASS BUILDERS

A series of technique book/CD packages created for the purposeful building and development of your chops. Each volume is written by an expert in that particular technique. And with the inclusion of audio, the added dimension of hearing exactly how to play particular grooves and techniques make these truly like private lessons.

BASS AEROBICS
by Jon Liebman
00696437 Book/Online Audio $19.99

**BASS FITNESS –
AN EXERCISING HANDBOOK**
by Josquin des Prés
00660177 .... $10.99

BASS FOR BEGINNERS
by Glenn Letsch
00695099 Book/CD Pack.. $19.95

BASS GROOVES
by Jon Liebman
00696028 Book/Online Audio $19.99

BASS IMPROVISATION
by Ed Friedland
00695164 Book/Online Audio $17.95

BLUES BASS
by Jon Liebman
00695235 Book/CD Pack.. $19.95

BUILDING ROCK BASS LINES
by Ed Friedland
00695692 Book/CD Pack.. $17.95

BUILDING WALKING BASS LINES
by Ed Friedland
00695008 Book/Online Audio $19.99

**RON CARTER –
BUILDING JAZZ BASS LINES**
00841240 Book/CD Pack.. $19.95

DICTIONARY OF BASS GROOVES
by Sean Malone
00695266 Book/Online Audio $14.95

EXPANDING WALKING BASS LINES
by Ed Friedland
00695026 Book/CD Pack.. $19.95

**FINGERBOARD HARMONY
FOR BASS**
by Gary Willis
00695043 Book/Online Audio $17.95

FUNK BASS
by Jon Liebman
00699348 Book/CD Pack.. $19.99

FUNK/FUSION BASS
by Jon Liebman
00696553 Book/CD Pack.. $19.95

HIP-HOP BASS
by Josquin des Prés
00695589 Book/CD Pack.. $15.99

JAZZ BASS
by Ed Friedland
00695084 Book/Online Audio $17.99

**JERRY JEMMOTT –
BLUES AND RHYTHM &
BLUES BASS TECHNIQUE**
00695176 Book/CD Pack.. $17.95

JUMP 'N' BLUES BASS
by Keith Rosier
00695292 Book/CD Pack.. $16.95

**THE LOST ART OF
COUNTRY BASS**
by Keith Rosier
00695107 Book/CD Pack.. $19.95

**PENTATONIC SCALES
FOR BASS**
by Ed Friedland
00696224 Book/Online Audio $19.99

REGGAE BASS
by Ed Friedland
00695163 Book/Online Audio $16.95

'70S FUNK & DISCO BASS
by Josquin des Prés
00695614 Book/Online Audio $16.99

**SIMPLIFIED SIGHT-READING
FOR BASS**
by Josquin des Prés
00695085 Book/Online Audio $17.99

6-STRING BASSICS
by David Gross
00695221 Book/CD Pack.. $12.95

www.halleonard.com

Hal•Leonard® BASS PLAY-ALONG

AUDIO ACCESS INCLUDED

The Bass Play-Along™ Series will help you play your favorite songs quickly and easily! Just follow the tab, listen to the CD or online audio to hear how the bass should sound, and then play along using the separate backing tracks. The melody and lyrics are also included in the book in case you want to sing, or to simply help you follow along. The audio files are enhanced so you can adjust the recording to any tempo without changing pitch!

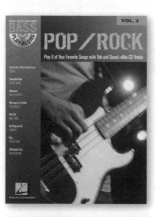

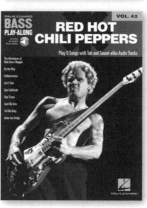

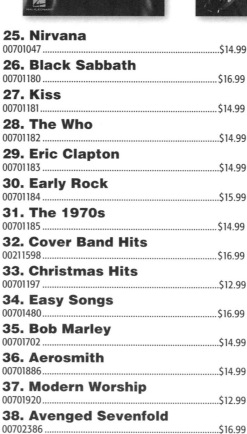

1. Rock
00699674 ....$14.99

2. R&B
00699675 ....$15.99

3. Pop/Rock
00699677 ....$12.95

4. '90s Rock
00699679 ....$14.99

5. Funk
00699680 ....$15.99

6. Classic Rock
00699678 ....$14.99

7. Hard Rock
00699676 ....$14.95

9. Blues
00699817 ....$14.99

10. Jimi Hendrix Smash Hits
00699815 ....$17.99

11. Country
00699818 ....$12.95

12. Punk Classics
00699814 ....$12.99

13. Lennon & McCartney
00699816 ....$14.99

14. Modern Rock
00699821 ....$14.99

15. Mainstream Rock
00699822 ....$14.99

16. '80s Metal
00699825 ....$16.99

17. Pop Metal
00699826 ....$14.99

18. Blues Rock
00699828 ....$14.99

19. Steely Dan
00700203 ....$16.99

20. The Police
00700270 ....$15.99

21. Rock Band – Modern Rock
00700705 ....$14.95

**23. Pink Floyd –
Dark Side of The Moon**
00700847 ....$15.99

24. Weezer
00700960 ....$14.99

25. Nirvana
00701047 ....$14.99

26. Black Sabbath
00701180 ....$16.99

27. Kiss
00701181 ....$14.99

28. The Who
00701182 ....$14.99

29. Eric Clapton
00701183 ....$14.99

30. Early Rock
00701184 ....$15.99

31. The 1970s
00701185 ....$14.99

32. Cover Band Hits
00211598 ....$16.99

33. Christmas Hits
00701197 ....$12.99

34. Easy Songs
00701480 ....$16.99

35. Bob Marley
00701702 ....$14.99

36. Aerosmith
00701886 ....$14.99

37. Modern Worship
00701920 ....$12.99

38. Avenged Sevenfold
00702386 ....$16.99

40. AC/DC
14041594 ....$16.99

41. U2
00702582 ....$16.99

42. Red Hot Chili Peppers
00702991 ....$19.99

43. Paul McCartney
00703079 ....$17.99

44. Megadeth
00703080 ....$16.99

45. Slipknot
00703201 ....$16.99

46. Best Bass Lines Ever
00103359 ....$17.99

47. Dream Theater
00111940 ....$24.99

48. James Brown
00117421 ....$16.99

49. Eagles
00119936 ....$17.99

50. Jaco Pastorius
00128407 ....$17.99

51. Stevie Ray Vaughan
00146154 ....$16.99

52. Cream
00146159 ....$17.99